P9-CRC-714

I Have Asthma

Text: **Jennifer Moore-Mallinos** / Illustrations: **Rosa M. Curto**

BARRON'S

I Have Asthma!

There are more than six million kids with asthma in the United States and Canada, and I am one of them. I found out I had asthma last summer, during soccer practice. It was a hot day and we were doing a lot of running. At first I thought I was just tired, but then I started having trouble breathing, and I couldn't stop coughing. I felt like I couldn't get enough air. I panicked!

FEB 2 1 2008

From across the field, Mom and Dad must have seen me struggling to catch my breath, because before I knew it they were standing right next to me. I never knew my parents could run that fast! They told me that I had to go to the hospital.

While Dad drove us to the hospital, Mom sat in the backseat next to me and tried to calm me down. Mom told me to close my eyes and take slow deep breaths. At first it was hard to do, and I didn't think it was going to help. Then after awhile it started to work, and I was able to breathe better.

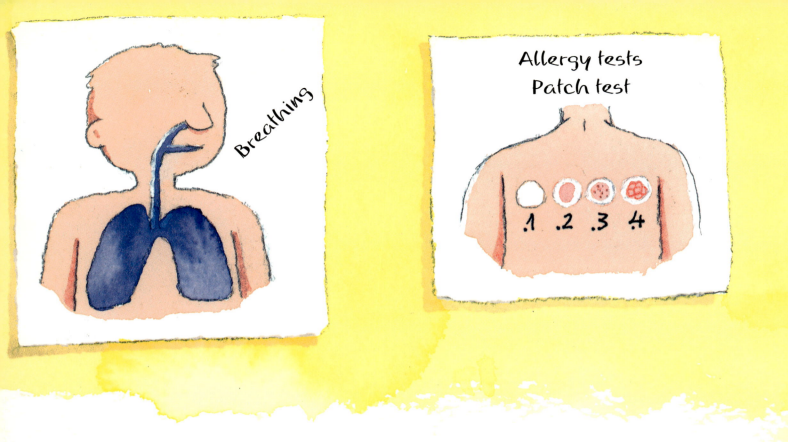

Breathing

Allergy tests
Patch test

.1 .2 .3 .4

Even though the hospital wasn't that far from the soccer field, it felt like it took forever to get there. As soon as we arrived, the doctor came to see me right away. The doctor told me that I was having an asthma attack and that I needed special medicine to help me breathe.

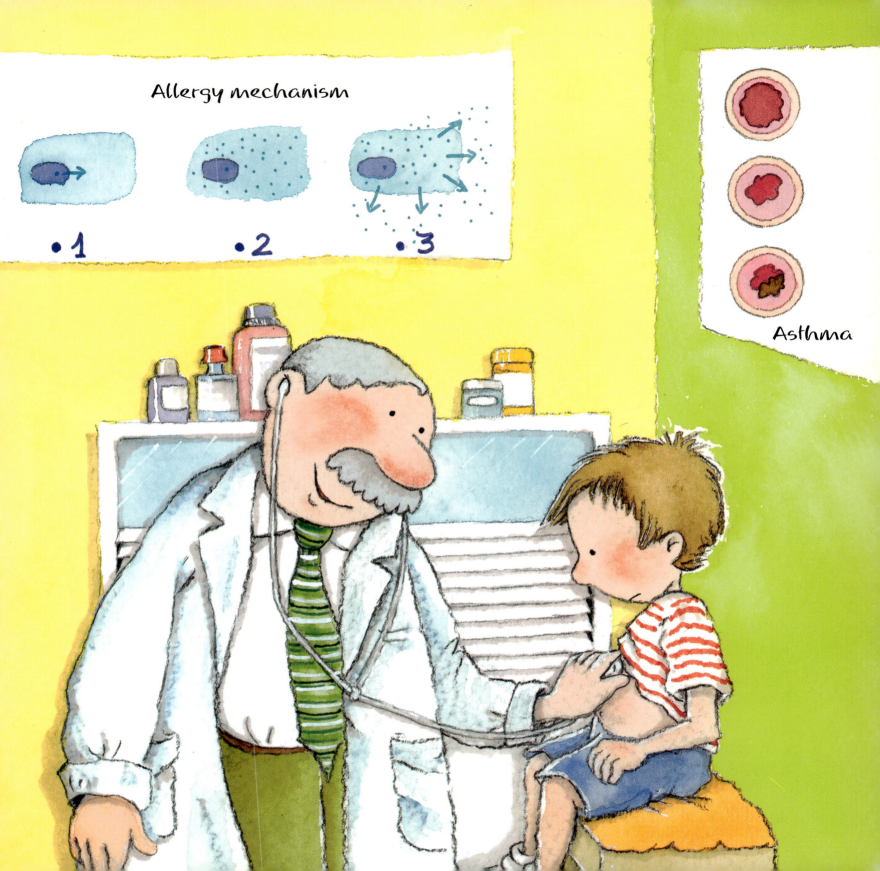

Allergy mechanism

•1 •2 •3

Asthma

The medicine the doctor gave me was different from any other medication I ever had. It wasn't like the flavored medicine you get when you have a cold, and it wasn't a pill either. Instead, it was medicine that I breathed in through my mouth using a small thing called an inhaler. The medicine didn't really have a flavor and it was easier than swallowing a pill, so I was happy.

Just before we left the hospital, the doctor explained what had happened to me. The reason I was coughing so hard and having difficulty breathing was because the air I breathed in was having trouble getting to my lungs. The tube that takes the air to my lungs was swollen. The medicine helped me because it took away some of the swelling in the tube.

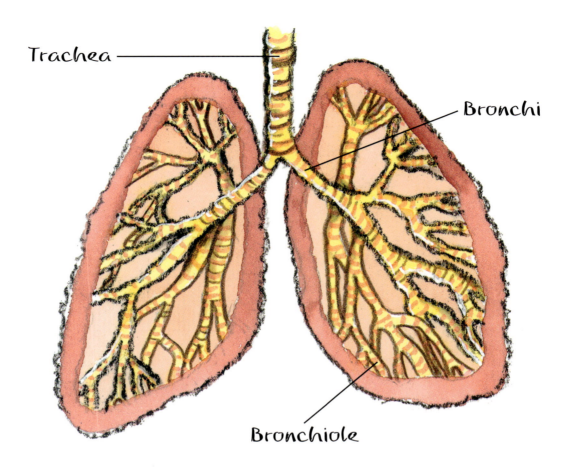

Trachea

Bronchi

Bronchiole

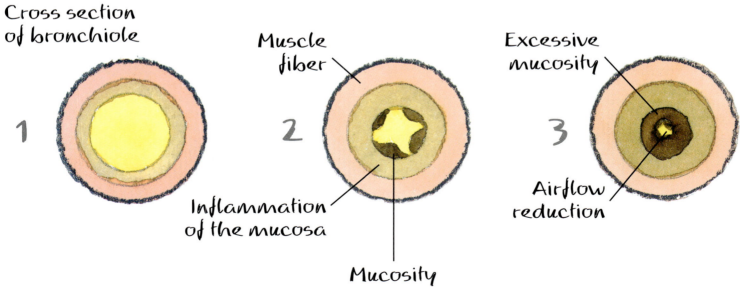

Cross section
of bronchiole

Muscle
fiber

Excessive
mucosity

1

2

3

Inflammation
of the mucosa

Mucosity

Airflow
reduction

On our way home from the hospital, Dad asked if I wanted to stop by the field to see if the team was still practicing. I wasn't sure I was ready to see my team. I was scared that, once they found out I had asthma, they wouldn't want to be friends with me anymore. But before I could say NO, Dad pulled into the parking lot and started beeping the horn.

When the team saw that it was us, everybody stopped practicing and ran to the parking lot. While Mom and Dad got out of the car, I stayed in and waited, with the windows closed. I thought if I waited long enough, they would leave me alone and go back to the field. But they didn't! Instead, they started cheering and calling my name. I had no choice but to get out of the car.

Everybody was happy to see me! The whole team, even my coach, gave me a hug. With all the excitement, I almost forgot I had asthma. I was just like the other kids again. But then my coach asked if I wanted to finish the practice with the team. I didn't want to be the one to tell them that I couldn't play soccer anymore, so I looked to my parents for their help to break the news.

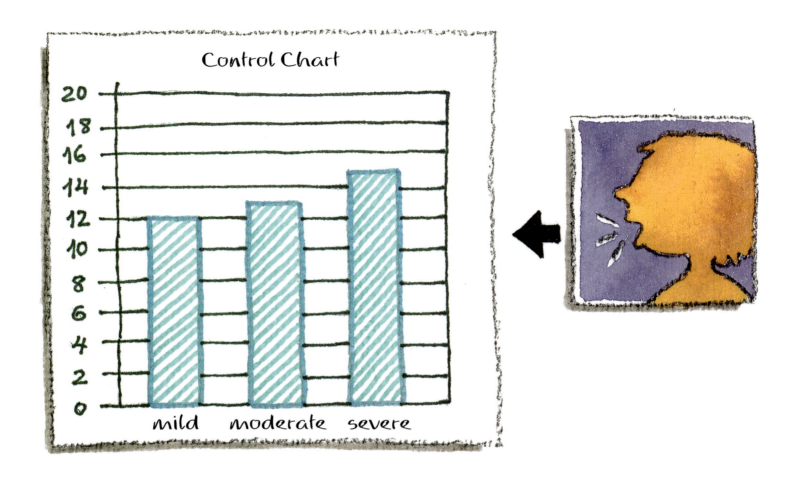

Control Chart

mild   moderate   severe

Instead, my parents told me that the doctor thought
it was probably okay for me to keep playing soccer
as long as I took my medicine before I played and
if I started coughing or had trouble breathing.
I was glad that I could keep playing soccer,
but I was scared. I didn't want anybody to
know I had asthma. I didn't know what to do.

While I was trying to decide, one of my teammates came over to me and quietly asked if I had asthma. When I said that I did, he told me that he had asthma, too! I was so surprised! How could the fastest runner on our team have asthma?

My teammate told me that he's had asthma since he was really little. He said he can still do all the things he loves to do, like play soccer, as long as he uses his inhaler before practice and games to help stop the asthma from starting. Just in case he starts coughing or has trouble breathing, he brings his inhaler with him wherever he goes.

Since that day, I've met a lot of kids who have asthma, just like I do. Some kids are even born with it. Did you know that dust and pollution can cause asthma for some kids? For others, it could be the weather or even exercise. I know more about asthma now then ever before, and there's still a lot to learn, but now it doesn't seem so scary to me anymore.

I still play soccer with my team and I love it! And no matter where I go, I always make sure I have my inhaler with me. A lot of kids have asthma, but having asthma doesn't have to mean that we have to stop being a kid or stop having fun!

Activities

Precautionary Measures

All allergy symptoms may get better with medical treatment, although prevention is the best policy. Doctors say that the best prevention is to avoid exposure to the elements that trigger allergy reactions. Although this is not always possible, you can reduce their effects and make symptoms easier to bear.

Here are ten pieces of advice to help you feel better:

1 Wash your hands and face as often as you can. Without realizing it, you may have been in a place full of dust or pollen, and this may trigger an attack. Keep yourself clean all the time.

2 During the period of pollination, avoid going outdoors between five and ten in the morning and seven and ten at night. The countryside, gardens, and parks are places where there is a lot of dust. Try not to lie down on the grass and go away from areas where they are mowing lawns or trimming bushes.

3 Days that are sunny, dry, and windy are the worst for people with allergies, because that's when the concentration of pollen is highest.

4 Apparently, pollination lasts longer in the mountains than at the seashore, because the sea breezes prevent the concentration of pollen and dust.

5 Avoid physical exercise in the early hours of the morning—better do it in the evening. The best sport for you is swimming, because you practice it in a dust-free environment.

6 Home cleansers may contain chemicals that produce allergic reactions or temporary breathing problems. Try not to stay in rooms where they are using these products.

7 Avoid fluffy toys because they may accumulate a lot of dust as well as mites. If you have a teddy bear, have someone wash it frequently in the washing machine.

8 Keep your bedroom window closed at night, because most plants release their pollen at that time.

9 When you are in the car, keep the windows up to avoid breathing air that is full of pollen.

10 Before you eat something you don't know, ask if it contains anything that may cause an allergic reaction.

Let's Be Detectives

As we learned in the text, there are many kids who have asthma. In fact, there are probably a lot of kids in your school who have it.

Let's pretend we are detectives…let's find out exactly how many kids in your school have asthma!

The best way to get information from a large number of people, like the kids in your school, is to use a survey. A survey is a list of questions about a subject, for example, asthma. Surveys are a great way to get a lot of information about a certain topic.

When preparing your list of questions, think about the information you need. For example, are there more boys than girls with asthma—or the other way around—more girls than boys with asthma?

When you prepare your questions try to involve kids who don't have asthma. For example, it may be interesting to find out what do kids without asthma (and even teachers) know about this disease. Are there books in your school library about asthma? What happens in gym class when a kid with asthma has to sit out? Do the other kids feel that such a boy or girl is getting special treatment, or do the kids understand that people with asthma may need to rest more often?

The results should be very interesting. Perhaps you will learn that there are very few kids in your school who have asthma or maybe there are more kids with asthma than you originally thought. The results of your survey might even show that few people (both kids and teachers) know very much about asthma. Maybe teaching people about asthma is a good idea.

An Inhaler Pouch

Having to carry your inhaler around everywhere you go can be a drag. How many times have you lost your inhaler at the bottom of your backpack? And let's face it, carrying your inhaler in your pants pocket can be uncomfortable!

So let's design your very own inhaler pouch. Not only will your pouch help you keep track of your inhaler, but it will make it easier for you to take your medicine anywhere you go!

4 For those of you who would like the pouch to have a handle, simply cut out a strip of material, any length you prefer. Attach each end to each side of your pouch. You can use fabric glue or a needle and thread to attach the handle.

Now it's time to decorate your pouch. Perhaps you would like to use glitter glue, or colorful markers. Whatever you choose to use, be creative and have fun!

How to make your very own pouch

1 With the help from an adult, cut your material into a rectangular shape approximately 12 × 9 inches. You may want to use scissors with either a straight edge or a fancy edge. You choose!

2 Fold the material in half.

3 Glue or sew both sides of the folded edges. DO NOT glue or sew the top of the shape. Please note: If you choose to use glue allow enough time for the glue to dry before you move to the next step.
With help from an adult, sew a large button in the middle of the inside top part of the pouch. On the other side, directly opposite the button, cut a small, straight line. This will be the buttonhole.

1

2

3

4

Guidelines to parents

The purpose of this book is to acknowledge the prevalence of asthma among children and to recognize some of the realities children with asthma may experience.

Being diagnosed with asthma can be scary for many children and their parents. However, some of these anxieties and fears can be eased by simply knowing more about the disease and how to treat it. It's amazing what a little insight and knowledge can do to make us feel more in control!

Although there are several commonalities among asthma sufferers, each child's experience can differ significantly. Not only can a child's symptoms vary in severity, but his or her willingness to manage them may also be different at times.

As we learned in the text, it's important that all children attempt to control their asthma. Learning to take their medication and to carry their inhalers at all times are easy ways for children to gain a sense of control over the disease. This also gives them the opportunity and the freedom to feel like normal kids most of the time.

We hope that this book leaves you with a better understanding of what asthma is, and that it helps eliminate any stigma associated with the disease.

The following information was obtained from the American Lung Association. Please note that it represents only a small part of a vast amount of information available. Additional research may be beneficial in acquiring a more complete understanding of asthma.

Kids and asthma

Did you know that asthma is one of the most common chronic (lasting) children diseases? In fact, more than six million U.S. and Canadian kids under the age of 18 years suffer from asthma. The word "asthma" comes from the Greek meaning to "breathe hard."

What is asthma?

Asthma is an inflammation or swelling of the airways. When the airways become inflamed or swollen, they become obstructed to a certain degree and cause excessive coughing and wheezing. Many complain of tightness in the chest, as if a great weight is put on their chest.

Can asthma be cured?

Asthma cannot be cured, but it can almost always be controlled. That's why it's so important to understand what asthma is, to know its signs and symptoms, and what can trigger it or increase it.

Signs and symptoms of asthma

Asthma does not affect kids all the time. Usually, when asthma is triggered it results in an asthmatic episode in which the airways narrow. When this happens, breathing becomes difficult. Other signs and symptoms of asthma include coughing, wheezing, continuously runny nose, tightness in the chest, and increased difficulty in breathing.

What triggers asthma?

Some things that can trigger or increase asthma are exercise, flu, dust and dust mites, allergies, irritants, weather, and even emotions.

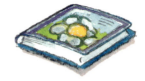

Infections

In many children, an asthma attack may be caused by a simple cold.

Physical exercise

In 80% of kids with asthma, running can trigger asthma. However, if asthma medication (bronchodilators) is used before exercise, most asthma episodes can be prevented. Running during extended periods (especially in cold weather), the allergy season, or a preexisting cold often are likely causes of asthma for some kids.

Dust at home

Did you know that there are tiny bugs that live in your house called dust mites? As their name implies, they love to live in dusty places. Dust mites can be found in furniture, carpets, drapes, pillows, and even on stuffed animals.

Allergy

For many kids, asthma symptoms can be initiated by allergies. Some allergy triggers include dust, pollen from flowers, grass, certain foods, and animal hair.

Irritants

Irritants such as cigarette smoke, air pollution, and household cleaners can all trigger reactions such as coughing, wheezing, difficult breathing, and runny nose.

Weather

Children with asthma seem to be more sensitive to cold weather, as it can cause asthma symptoms to appear.

Emotions

Did you know that a child's breathing is faster when he or she has been crying, laughing hard, or yelling? Even feeling scared, angry, or even frustrated can cause an asthmatic episode.

Types of asthma

There are two main types of asthma triggers: allergic (extrinsic) and non-allergic (intrinsic).
Some allergic triggers include dust, pollen, and animal hair, whereas non-allergic triggers may include cigarette smoke, exercise, wood, pollution, and even changes in the weather.
Avoiding these triggers can prevent asthma from starting.
Most childhood asthma is considered extrinsic and occurs more often in boys than girls.

Other types of asthma

Other types of asthma include exercise-induced asthma, bronchial asthma, nocturnal asthma, and seasonal asthma.

Asthma medication

The two medications most often given to children with asthma are anti-inflammatory drugs (preventive medication) and bronchodilators (relieving medication). Anti-inflammatory medications help reduce the swelling in the airway, whereas bronchodilators dilate the airways and relax the bronchial muscle. These medications are most often taken by breathing the medicine in through an inhaler.
For most kids, an asthmatic episode can be avoided by taking medicine in the morning and before going to bed. These are called preventive specifics. At other times, if the child is coughing and wheezing, he or she may take medications that will facilitate breathing. These are called relieving medications.

I HAVE ASTHMA

Text: **Jennifer Moore-Mallinos**
Illustrations: **Rosa M. Curto**

First edition for the United States and Canada published
in 2007 by Barron's Educational Series, Inc.
Original title of the book in Spanish: *Tengo asma.*

© Copyright 2007 by Gemser Publications, S.L.
C/Castell, 38; Teià (08329) Barcelona, Spain (World Rights)
Tel. 93 540 13 53
E-mail info@mercedesros.com

All inquiries should be addressed to:
Barron's Educational Series, Inc.
250 Wireless Boulevard
Hauppauge, New York 11788
http://www.barronseduc.com

ISBN-13: 978-0-7641-3785-3
ISBN-10: 0-7641-3785-9
Library of Congress Control Number 2006938823

Printed in China
9 8 7 6 5 4 3 2 1

All rights reserved. No part of this book may be reproduced in
any form, by photostat, microfilm, xerography, or any other
means, or incorporated into any information retrieval
system, electronic or mechanical, without the
written permission of the copyright owner.